Contents

Contents

Defence Conversion and Conventional Arms Control after the Cold War

Richard Latter

July 1992

WILTON PARK PAPER 58

Conference Report based on Wilton Park Arms Control Seminar II, organised in co-operation with The Roosevelt Institute: 10–12 June 1992. Conventional Arms control and Defence Conversion in the 1990s.

LONDON: HMSO

ISBN 0 11 701711 6
ISSN 0953–8542

1   Introduction

The end of the Cold War confrontation between the Soviet Empire and a US-led NATO has prompted the collapse of the former and reductions in the armed forces and military spending of the latter. In both regions political commitments have been made to reduce defence spending; real cuts are already occurring, and a substantial reduction in domestic markets for defence equipment seems assured. This welcome change poses problems for Western defence industries and companies; in order to remain in business and to make continued profits they have to re-assess future military needs, adjust research and development activity, and efficiently use excess capacity by converting facilities and re-training work-forces to produce non-military goods competitive in the civilian market. Failure to convert effectively to 'civilian' production will necessitate plant closures and laying off workers. Western governments are also concerned; they have to decide whether to give financial support to companies' conversion efforts, to provide special assistance for the newly unemployed resulting from factory closures, and to deal with resulting social distress.

In the former Soviet Union and former Warsaw Pact states these problems are compounded by the general breakdown of economic activity and trade, and by problems associated with efforts to replace the old centralised economic system by market economies. In the Soviet Union in particular reducing the huge military-industrial complex and redirecting much of its activity towards civilian production is a massive problem. While Western-style capitalist defence companies did not exist in the former Communist states, individual factories and production facilities face similar problems to their Western counterparts.

What are the implications for arms control? Will the reduction in size of local markets lead to reductions in the amounts and types of military equipment produced, or will production levels be maintained through exports? The second option clearly has its attractions for both Western companies and producers in the East, at least in the short term while they seek to restructure their operations; indeed export earnings may fund the conversion required. Yet, it remains to be seen whether the international market outside North America and Europe will be sufficiently large to take up anticipated 'over-production'.

It is also important to stress that the quantities of armaments exported are not the sole concern; the effect of declining domestic markets on the *quality* of armaments exported is a crucial factor: for example, exports of missiles, nuclear, chemical and biological weapons technologies and conventional high technology, such as STEALTH or Cruise missile guidance systems, would be highly de-stabilising in areas of regional conflict. It remains to be seen whether recent Cold War adversaries can agree to act together to restrict effectively such exports.

It is important for the West to establish how far it wishes to co-operate economically with Russia and other East European states to encourage them to restrict their exports; for example, it is unclear how far, and how, the West should intervene in the reconstruction of Eastern economies to facilitate conversion of defence industries. Of course, the importance of rapid economic reconstruction to building political and social stability in Eastern Europe can not be under-estimated. Yet, if the West seeks 'stability', and offers aid to this end, can it also link aid to the introduction of democracy, of market-oriented policies, and of 'correct' financial policies? Aid conditionality has been stressed, for example by the Bush Administration, when pressing the newly-independent East European states to ratify and implement the CFE Agreement and, where appropriate, START nuclear agreements. It remains to be seen whether aid can and will be withheld in the name of arms control, when the need for economic reconstruction is so important. In a period of confusion it is certain that progress on democratisation and on building a market economy, in Russia for example, will not be uniform and setbacks will occur. In such situations there may not always be a strong case for withholding economic assistance provided that the *long-term* trend remains positive. Thus, while conditionality may be valuable it should not be implemented so rigidly that the West allows the states of the East to collapse into war and anarchy.

The fact remains that the effectiveness of Western aid will be dependent upon local efforts to restructure national economies and to proceed effectively with defence conversion. The alternatives in the East are stark. Conversion at best means the effective, alternative use of equipment and skills to meet non-defence needs in domestic or international markets. If this is not possible defence enterprises can only continue to function by supplementing their reduced domestic sales with exports. The third alternative is closure. Either of the last two options is disastrous, the one for the international community and the other for the national or local community involved. The need is to establish how the peoples and economies of East and West can successfully undertake defence conversion, recognising that while they share similar problems each may require a different solution given the differences between their economic systems and performances.

2   Defence Conversion in the West

The reduction in defence spending in Western countries has prompted three key questions: how defence companies may best react, what action should be taken by governments, and how should the 'peace dividend' be spent?

The United States

Reductions in defence spending are taking place against the background of a US recession in which 'official' unemployment is set at 7.5 per cent, and unofficial figures reach 10 per cent, when 'the disenchanted' who are no longer seeking work are included. The effects of the recession are particularly marked in certain States and in many of these defence industries form an important component in the local economy. For these reasons the curtailing of a number of defence programmes has been resisted, not least by interested Congressmen, supported by company lobbying. In addition, a genuine discussion is developing over the need for an accurate assessment of risks and threats and a clear military doctrine and strategy to guide future procurement decisions. The lack of such clear guidance has been offered as a reason for slowing the reduction of military expenditure.

In spite of such problems and reservations, substantial cuts in US military spending are occurring and are planned for the future. The numbers of military personnel are being cut, procurement programmes ended and production runs, for example for the STEALTH bomber, severely cut back. Since 1986 defence spending has fallen by 2–3 per cent per year in real terms. It is estimated that 1.3 million workers will be 'released' into the civilian economy as a result of these cuts. The reactions of defence companies to these changes are being driven by market principles and involve little direct government intervention.

A further consolidation of defence companies is occurring in the United States; the current situation in which ten companies utilise 30 per cent of the US Defence budget and the top 100 companies utilise 75 per cent is being reinforced by mergers and acquisitions. In addition, some companies are seeking to globalise further their operations by buying foreign companies or entering into co-operation agreements with them; this makes good sense in an increasingly global market although American companies have experienced problems in raising sufficient funds to finance desired acquisitions, given the reticence of US and Japanese financial institutions.

US companies are seeking to break down further the barriers between defence and non-defence technology, noting that while defence technology has not proved generally usable in civilian contexts a great deal of civilian technology, particularly in computing, is applicable to defence. They note that the US Department of Defence is now a net user of civilian R&D and due notice has been taken of recent arguments that the Japanese economic miracle has been made possible in part by Japanese companies concentrating their R&D efforts in the civilian sector rather than on defence. As a result companies are seeking to diversify into 'civilian' production. Many companies have also slimmed down their defence operations by concentrating on key areas where they are able to dominate the market and have particularly strong skills. 'Conversion' in the sense of finding alternative uses for existing assets plays a relatively *small* part in this adjustment process.

The worry for the US Government is that company actions based purely on market considerations may have adverse results in a future US reliance on foreign suppliers, a diminution of the US defence technology base, and rising unemployment. Yet the Bush Administration does not appear to have been persuaded that these consequences are sufficiently serious to merit strong government intervention and defence reductions appear likely to continue apace. Concern about these issues is concentrated in the Congress, where foreign acquistions of US companies have been resisted and efforts to keep production lines open have been strenuous. Yet, in general, the Administration appears to be prepared for the market to determine events. Some US observers question this approach; for example, the issue of what industrial capability should be protected and maintained domestically is being hotly debated, centering on such cases as the "sale of LTV Corp's Missile and Aircraft Divisions ... (where) Lockheed and Martin Marietta were outbid for the assets which are being sold to France's Thompson-CSF and a Washington-based investment group, the Carlisle Group. So far, the US Government has done nothing to stop the sale, although some see it as a national security asset being sold to a foreign company, and ultimately, a foreign government.'[1]

Administration initiatives have been limited to placing an increased emphasis on R&D programmes in the defence budget and encouraging inclusion of dual-use techology in defence

---

[1] Sharon Hobson, "Picking Your Partner. Globalisation of the Defence Industry has now Evolved Beyond Co-production and Offset Arrangements", *Jane's Defence Weekly*, Vol. 18 No. 1, 4 July 1992, p. 43.

programmes. Modest proposals to meet corporations' problems have included the granting of tax credits to some companies, retraining programmes for workforces and limited direct assistance to small contractors, but it is unclear whether these ideas will be implemented. The real emphasis in the US political debate is not on conversion and restructuring of company activities, which many believe are best left to the companies themselves, but rather on how best to exploit the 'peace dividend'.

Suggestions vary widely; some groups advocate the use of defence savings to reduce the US Government budget deficit and national debt, arguing that this will stimulate the economy, provide more jobs and generate an economic climate in which restructured defence companies can prosper. Others argue for the redirection of funds, and re-allocation of manpower and skills to meet chronic domestic problems: the decaying inner-cities, racial tensions, and the poverty of the American under-class. For example, Senator Sam Nunn, the Chairman of the Armed Services Committee, has noted: "We are still battling at home drugs, poverty, urban decay, lack of self-esteem, unemployment and racism ... The military cannot solve these problems ... but I am totally convinced that there is a proper and important role the armed forces can play in addressing these pressing issues."[2] His specific proposals include: using "enlisted personnel and officers, especially from minority groups, as 'role models' ... in community service programs among young people whose families have been weakened by poverty, drugs and crime; (giving) assistance ... in renovating public housing, schools and recreation facilities and in providing temporary facilities, such as a replacement for the women's and children's nutrition centre that was destroyed in the Los Angeles riots; ...recruiting disadvantaged students for existing summer jobs at military installations; ... using military medical personnel and facilities to provide infant vaccinations and other basic services to people with no other access to them."[3]

---

[2] Allan Dewar, "Re-cycling US Troops: A Broad At-Home Plan. Nunn Proposes Military Help Range from Immunisation to New Housing", *International Herald Tribune,* 25 June 1992.
[3] *Ibid.*

There is little doubt that such 'social' issues will dominate the US political agenda over the next few years and influence significantly the debate on the re-allocation of resources made available by defence reductions. However, it is unclear whether a direct re-allocation of *all* such resources would suffice to meet these problems. The infusions of capital and manpower required are such that a more wide-ranging re-structuring of US Government spending is required: the budget deficit problem has to be solved, taxes may have to rise, no matter how unpopular, and even deeper cuts in US defence spending may be required. Indeed, it is not too fanciful to suggest that this process could lead to the eventual total withdrawal of US military forces from Europe. This is a scenario which Europeans would do well to bear in mind as their defence industries seek to adjust to reduced European defence spending.

Western Europe

The US pattern of force reductions, defence cuts and the cancellation of defence projects has been broadly followed in Western Europe. Domestic implications are similar; for example, the UK debate about continuing the European Fighter Aircraft (EFA) project, following German withdrawal, is dominated by concerns about the 40,000 jobs involved, maintaining the country's technological base, and the impact on local economies. However, Europe differs from the US in that there is a significant international dimension to the problem, given the involvement of groups of countries in multi-national defence projects; adjusting to national defence cuts involves government-to-government negotiations and associated pressures.

Thus far national interests appear to be dominating this inter-action, as exemplified in the German withdrawal from the EFA project, and the UK choice of Challenger II as the British Army's new main battle tank. Such decisions are being made in an environment framed by nationally-based reduction programmes; for example, the projected 5.5 per cent reduction in UK spending in real terms by 1994–95 will be structured with due reference to the fact that "Britain still retains worldwide responsibilities and the annual defence white paper ... (is) to reflect this wider security role."[4] In contrast "Germany's withdrawal from the production phase of the £20 billion EFA programme is not just on financial grounds. The Bonn Government views its security role from a totally different aspect. Germany has not deployed its fighter aircraft abroad since the Second World War. Britain, however, has frequently been called upon to deploy aircraft out of the NATO area, most recently during the Gulf War, and still designs fighter planes capable of a global security role."[5] Determination to retain effective national defence capabilities in Finland and Sweden is such that *no* reductions in defence spending are projected in the near future.

West European companies have reacted to changing circumstances by seeking to increase market share, and making greater use of economies of scale through a series of mergers and acquisitions. They have been particularly active in purchasing US companies in an effort to globalise their operations. Thus, for example: "Pushed by the single European market and shrinking defence budgets, conglomerates such as GEC-Marconi, Thompson-CSF and Deutsche Aerospace (DASA), are buying and selling companies as their requirements dictate, and even co-operating among themselves in joint ventures in an effort to compete successfully in a shrunken market place."[6] The activities of these companies are particularly important in Western Europe, where governments continue to stress the importance of *national* security and defence policies, notwithstanding the rather weak commitments to joint policy in the Maastricht Treaty.

The companies' activity "results ... (in) creation of huge transnational companies (which) some analysts feel may undermine

---

[4] Michael Evans, "Rifkind Underlines Britain's Role as Global Peacekeeper", *The Times,* 8 July 1992.

[5] *Ibid.*

[6] Sharon Hobson, "Picking Your Partner. Globalisation of the Defence Industry has now Evolved Beyond Co-production and Offset Arrangements", *Jane's Defence Weekly,* 4 July 1992, p. 43.

national security ... the re-structuring is being done on the basis of what most benefits individual companies. There are no overall national plans as to what sectors must be maintained or what technologies should be protected ... for example, while earlier collaboration projects such as the Tornado and Jaguar aircraft were initiated by the government which wanted to satisfy a defence requirement at the lowest cost, current collaborative projects, such as those initiated by Rolls-Royce, are for commercial reasons."[7] Some analysts fear that the ability of governments effectively to maintain national defence establishments is being undermined; it will no longer be possible for countries to have certainty of supply in times of crisis if they have to rely on foreign companies, for example for spares or ammunition.

These problems are recognised by West European governments but, as in the United States, they are doing little to change company policy; further mergers and co-operative ventures are certain given the increasing cost of projects and the strength of US competition: "US manufacturers were increasing their market share and accounted for 51 per cent of total deliveries last year, compared with 30 per cent in 1987."[8] The anticipated fierceness of competition between the US and Europe has implications for Russian, FSU and former WTO defence industries; their futures seem even more tenuous when faced with more competitive and more aggressive competition from Western companies in the world market.

3 Defence Conversion in the East

It is a widely trumpeted truism that East European economies are in chaos and that Russia in particular faces economic disaster because of: "the fall in production, the decline in foreign trade,

---

[7] *Ibid.*

[8] "Global spending down by 3 per cent", *Jane's Defence Weekly,* 27 June 1992, p. 1127.

the rise in inflation, and the shortage of Roubles."[9] Others point to different causes: "... the ills that Russian officials like to present as evidence of the mismanagement of reforms are not what need to be cured. The real malady is derived from the inflationary palliatives, unjustified pay rises, and soaring credits that have been applied to an economy which requires a fundamental restructuring that has not even started".[10] All agree, however, that significant improvements in economic performance are required to meet people's needs and aspirations; an essential precondition for the social and political stability which is needed to reinforce democracy and market-oriented policies.

Russia

The role to be played by defence 'conversion' in restructuring the Russian economy is critical given the size of the defence industry inherited from the Communist system; for example, 60 per cent of Russian engineering and 75 per cent of R&D, respectively, were for the Soviet military. Both financial and human resources must be redirected into the civilian sector if the general restructuring of the economy is to succeed. This is all the more important given the fact that the defence industry "represents the most capable part of the economy in terms of its ability to develop and produce goods of relatively high technology and quality. This capability owes much to the excellence of the industry's research and engineering personnel, and this in turn can be explained to a large extent by the existence of a well-developed system of specialist higher education, in particular a group of élite technical institutes responsible for training many of the defence sector's leading engineering and managerial staff."[11] Furthermore, "over many years highly capable research and design schools have consolidated, adept at finding effective solutions to problems in the

---

[9] Mary Dejevsky, "Yeltsin Plea for G7 Hand-out Veils Signs of Resilient Economy", *The Times,* 7 July 1992.
[10] *Ibid.*
[11] Julian Cooper, "Defence Industry Conversion in the East: the Relevance of Western Experience", paper presented at the NATO-Central and East European Countries Seminar on Defence Industry Conversion, Brussels, 20–22 May 1992.

absence of the full range of resource possibilities open to their Western counterparts."[12] Yet this highly capable defence industry exists in a relatively weak and inefficient economy and the market for its products has been severely reduced. Recent estimates indicate that military expenditure has fallen by 70 per cent in real terms.

How is change to be encouraged and managed? Soviet commentators have concentrated on the difficulties of financing such a change, stressing that effective transition will require high investment. Estimates of R150 billion over the next 5–7 years have been made. Sources for such financing are: the Russian state budget, which has allocated R40 billion to the task, hard currency earned by sales of plant to Western investors and/or arms sales, and foreign direct investment.

Russian efforts to earn hard currency are already under way. The transfer of rocket-engine technology to India is an example. "The troubled Russian defence sector badly needs to make this and other sales to earn hard currency and build up investment funds. At $250 million, the Indian sale is a small fraction of the defence establishment's 1992 goal of $5 billion worth of military equipment exports – a 64 per cent drop from last year. ... Russian officials, bristling from criticism by conservatives that they bend too easily to the whims of the West, are likely to fight back, arguing that the United States not only sells more weapons than any other country but also is spending millions of Pentagon Dollars promoting the US defence industry abroad."[13]

Russian exporters have much leeway to make up in the face of severe American competition: thus, while US sales increased in 1991, "The former Soviet Union accounted for 18 per cent of total sales, down from 39 per cent in 1987."[14] It is therefore unsurprising that the Russian defence industry is working hard to develop

---

[12] *Ibid.*
[13] "Worldgram, US News and World Report", 18 May 1992.
[14] "Global Spending Down by 3 per cent", *Jane's Defence Weekly,* 27 June 1992, p. 1127.

new markets. For example, it has been noted that Turkey, a NATO member, is considering buying $300 million worth of helicopter gunships and armoured vehicles from Russia. Even here uncertainty persists: "The feasibility of the purchase has been questioned by some Turkish defence industry officials, who foresee technical and logistic problems ... because of the uncertain future of the Russian defence industry."[15] There can be little doubt that Turkish officials will be giving due consideration to possible alternatives from Western suppliers, and indeed may yet take advantage of NATO 'cascading' to meet their needs, notwithstanding the concern of some NATO members about the uses to which the equipment may be put.

Whatever the success of Russian arms export drives, it is unclear whether these will generate sufficient hard currency to fund successful conversion. What role can foreign direct investment and Western aid be expected to play? Western reaction to Russian requests for large-scale financial assistance has been cautious; it is widely appreciated that such assistance can only be effective if a genuine reform of the Russian economic system is occurring. The problem is to ensure that aid given is not wasted or misappropriated during the current period of economic chaos; support should only be given where there is a good chance of success and needs cannot be met locally.

On the other hand, Western leaders are constrained by their desire to ensure that witholding Western aid does not of itself precipitate a crisis and the possible fall of the current reformist Russian leadership. For this reason the G7 leaders decided in Munich in early July 1992 to unlock a $1 billion credit from the IMF and to adopt a generous attitude to the deferrment of the former Soviet Union's debt repayments. Yet, Russian pressure for further Western investment continues: "Mr Yeltsin said that the $24 billion being offered through the IMF was insufficient to solve his country's problems and see through the reform package. He

---

[15] Lale Sariibrahimoglu, "Turkey Considers Russian Arms Buy", *Jane's Defence Weekly*, 11 July 1992, p. 12.

appealed to private investors to show courage and to invest now the IMF deal had been signed."[16] It is unlikely that Western governments will respond to such a request for a further massive infusion of funds; it is increasingly recognised that the Western governments' role should be limited to 'pump-priming' private investment and to assisting more directly in certain key sectors, for example transport, food distribution and storage.

A 'Marshall Plan' type programme seems unlikely to materialise and indeed some observers argue that major infusions of capital are unnecessary to convert former Soviet defence industries. The real needs are different. The Russian Government must establish a superstructure providing stable conditions within which businesses can work effectively. A comprehensive system of company law must be introduced. Taxation and foreign exchange regulations need to be established along with a sound banking system. Regional, local and borough development working groups, such as local chambers of commerce and industrial development agencies, need to be established to co-ordinate industrial regeneration at a local level.

Conversion has to be managed locally and with local resources; the role of the West will be to provide expertise, know-how and training to facilitate this work. At a broader level enterprises must be encouraged to assess the demand that exists in the local market place and use this as a basis for deciding what to produce and what to sell. In the early stages of the conversion process, enterprises may be better able to sell in the Russian and FSU markets than in the West, where their products will generally be uncompetitive. An incremental and small-scale approach is probably the best option. The successes of such projects will help to build confidence but this will take time.

There is no large-scale panacea to be derived from dramatic, wide-ranging programmes of Western aid or Russian legislation; while

---

[16] Robin Oakley and Ian Murray, "G7 Agrees on Aid for Yeltsin", *The Times,* 9 July 1992.

these may contribute to the creation of an environment less hostile to the evolution of capitalist enterprises, the human and financial resources required at the ground level will have to be furnished locally, with 'the West' furnishing expertise and training. It remains to be seen whether the Russian social and political systems are resilient enough to provide the stability needed for such gradual change to occur.

Central Europe

The defence industries of the former WTO countries of Central Europe constituted a far smaller sector than in the FSU. In addition they were primarily geared to exports. For example, Hungary exported 90–92 per cent of its defence production in the late 1990s. Central European defence industries were also less exclusively dependent upon defence work: only one-third of Czech defence companies, for example, had a defence dependency of 20 per cent or more. 'Civilian' enterprises carried on within defence industries included the production of heavy goods vehicles, aircraft and electrical goods. Nevertheless, the general collapse of centralised economies in Eastern Europe severely reduced their export markets, notably to the Soviet Union, and it is estimated that only 20–40 per cent of capacity remains in production.

The result is closures and rising unemployment, concentrated in vulnerable regions where the defence industry is concentrated. For example, the Czechoslovak defence industry was largely located in Slovakia and the current unemployment of 12 per cent in this region, compared with 4 per cent in the Czech lands, has been an important factor in the political disintegration of the state.

Conversion offers a possible means of arresting this decline. It is suggested that companies should concentrate on meeting local civilian needs and selling to the FSU as they will be better able to sell in these markets than in the West where higher quality Western products make competition difficult. Even this option will not be easy as the low quality and poor reliability of 'civilian' products produced by Central European defence industries may also undermine their competitiveness at home, as Western companies begin to sell in the East.

These difficulties have already forced a re-thinking of priorities and the early commitments, for example by President Havel, to cease military production and exports appear to be weakening. Sales of arms to the protagonists in the Yugoslav civil war, and of Czech tanks to Syria, demonstrate that Central European defence industries remain active in the international market. If conversion is not successful options for the industries include: a. retaining a military production capability and seeking to improve its quality and high-tech component; b. continuing exports of basic equipment using existing technology to fund modernisation at a later date; c. using facilities to destroy surplus equipment; d. developing links with Western companies to acquire infusions of capital and technology. If current trends continue it seems likely that defence factories will either close or continue with their existing defence oriented activity: any increase in current 'civilian' activity will be gradual.

While Western companies are likely to make decisions about co-operating with local companies on a commercial basis, Western governments continue to assess possible Western involvement in national security terms. For example, the oft-proposed ending of COCOM regulations, or at least their amendment to allow yet more exports of Western high-technology to Central Europe, can only be permitted if the technology transferred will not be used to develop more effective defence industries. These could compete with Western companies, increase arms sales and in the worst case supply revanchist nationalist regimes in the area which could threaten the West.

To avoid the evolution of such regimes, Western aid must remain conditional upon continuing progress towards democratic politics, market economies, and free and open societies. Differing assessments regarding the likelihood of such progress are influencing decisions on the level and nature of conditions to be placed on future Western aid.

Aid Conditionality

During the 1980s, Western aid donors have increasingly linked aid to the Third World with good government, economic structural adjustment, respect for human and minority rights, and environmental issues. These same principles must be applied to the FSU and Central Europe. Recently a further dimension has been added, initially by the Japanese Government, explicitly linking recipient countries' military expenditure with the provision of aid. Noting that the share of less developed countries in global arms imports amounted to over 75 per cent, and that the majority of arms transfers were being financed by military aid, donors increasingly call for the use of recipients' limited resources to promote development rather than to buy weapons. The Japanese Government has stressed that excessive military expenditure undermines efforts to make effective use of available local resources and aid; it has long been observed that aid allows the diversion of local funds from development to defence projects. Increasing numbers of countries including, for example, Germany and the United Kingdom, as well as the multilateral agencies such as the World Bank and the IMF, are making aid decisions with these factors in mind.

This sea-change in Western attitudes will impinge directly on Central and East European states. They will be under increasing pressure to limit domestic military 'consumption', and to reduce exports to Third World purchasers who are urged by donors to reduce military expenditure. The overall increase in global demand for aid, caused by the addition of East European demands, means that competition for aid will be fiercer, and potential recipients may be more susceptible to donor pressures.

However, implementation of aid conditionality is fraught with problems. Recipients may be resentful of donor pressure, if the donor nations are themselves over-armed, possess large military export industries, and intervene too strongly in what are perceived to be 'internal affairs'. At a more theoretical level, establishing precisely what levels of defence expenditure and equipment are 'adequate' for a recipient country may be problematical. Some of the most significant arms importing countries, for example the oil-rich Gulf States, are well able to finance substantial military purchases without Western aid. They in turn provide potentially rich markets for Russia and other East European states. Thus the effective leverage of the donor countries on both 'supplier and buyer' is not without limit. In such a situation the application of arms control agreements may offer a positive way forward, leading to a reduction in 'demand' by increasing military stability and predictability, improving crisis management, working to establish regional military balances, and ending or forestalling regional arms races by persuading sellers and buyers to restrict sales and purchases.

4 Implications for Arms Control

The prospects are poor for a significant reduction in the international arms trade through a 'supply-side' approach, via self-restraint, or by government restriction of arms industries. Western companies are re-organising and competing fiercely in the international market following domestic defence cuts; their Eastern counterparts are not adjusting well, but rather concentrating on what they know best and seeking to export their military products. Different circumstances are pushing both Eastern and Western suppliers in the same direction, and in neither case is government acting effectively to restrict exports. Indeed, backed by their governments, West European and US companies in particular have eagerly and successfully promoted arms sales to the Middle East following the Gulf War. In this situation it seems likely that only the size and nature of market demand will determine the levels and quality of arms traded.

Likely Future Markets

The value of the global arms trade is relatively small, representing only 50 per cent of US national military spending, and falling: "Global defence trade dropped sharply last year and was estimated at $22.1 billion (1990 dollars). This is roughly 25 per cent less than the previous year."[17] In addition the relative importance of regional markets is changing: "Middle Eastern nations accounted for 32 per cent of imports in 1982 against 21 per cent in 1991. Asia increased its share from 15 per cent in 1982 to 34 per cent last year."[18] African and Latin American purchases fell as a percentage of total less developed country purchases; indeed, 15 countries accounted for 75 per cent of the trade.

India and Pakistan, South Africa, Egypt and Israel, Thailand, and Taiwan featured strongly: all feel that the risk of military conflict with their neighbours is high and are little involved in regional arms control. The relatively small number of 'major' arms purchasers in the less developed world suggests a concentration of international effort to deal with their problems through a combination of supply-side restrictions and efforts to reduce demand through arms control initiatives.

Many argue that such an approach is too narrow. Problems caused by the arms trade are not directly proportionate to the numbers, quality and value of items traded; relatively small quantities of arms which are not 'state-of-the-art' can cause great turmoil. Although the number of wars registered by the Stockholm International Peace Research Institute (SIPRI) has fallen since 1990 from 33 to 30, the ferocity and damage inflicted in the remainder cannot be dismissed, and they do not all involve 'major' arms purchasers. For example, the flow of relatively unsophisticated arms into Yugoslavia has significantly affected the ability of each side to prosecute its aim; crude procurement procedures have sufficed to evade the international arms embargo. Thus, the international community cannot afford to concentrate on a few readily identified large-scale importers of arms. Attention must also be focused on the medium to small-scale purchasers.

---

[17] "Global Spending Down by 3 per cent", *Jane's Defence Weekly,* 27 June 1992, p. 1127.
[18] *Ibid.*

A number of these will be refitting their armed forces in the mid-1990s as equipment dating from the 1960s is phased out. In addition, many countries will be seeking to acquire the high-technology systems which performed so well during the Gulf War, and these purchases may stimulate qualitative arms races between near neighbours. Broader changes in the international environment may also lead to an upsurge of purchases. For example, the withdrawal of a permanent and active US presence in some regions of the world, because of the ending of the Cold War confrontation, may prompt allies to increase their defence capability in the belief that they will increasingly have to provide for their own security without US support.

Do these changes necessarily mean that the arms 'required' will be purchased from former Cold War protagonist countries? In the case of advanced weaponry, this is indeed likely to be the case given the general failure of Third World countries to develop their own military industrial capability. While only limited information is available, it seems clear that there has been no emergence of major arms producers in the Third World and, indeed, that the number may actually fall. In high-technology fields, Third World countries are unable to compete; for example, there is little innovation and local refinement of technology imported from the US, FSU and Europe. This situation is unlikely to change in the near future given the lack of sustained government support for local industries (eg through procurement), the difficulty of defence-related technological development in economies with only a low-level high-tech capability, and the existence of technology 'blocks' which companies' technicians are unable to solve.

Two factors run counter to this general trend. The availability of skilled technicians from the Soviet bloc to work in Third World countries is already a Western concern. In addition, Western companies, through their increasing globalisation, inevitably are involved in 'off-shore' production, sometimes of complete systems but more usually of components and dual-use technology items. The difficulties of controlling know-how and technology transfer will increase.

While the development of the UN data base on transfers of conventional weapons, in certain limited categories, is a step in the right direction, the supply-side control of conventional weapons remains a complicated and as yet under-resourced activity. The considerable economic weight of Western companies and in the future their Eastern counterparts, will make control even more difficult. This is why many argue that arms control efforts should concentrate upon reducing the demand for weapons systems. Others doubt the efficacy of such an approach, pointing to the Middle East as an example.

The Middle East

Some progress has been made on Middle Eastern problems which have fuelled arms races in the past. The Arab-Israeli peace process may be reinforced by the election of a new Israeli government. The defeat of Iraq is leading to the destruction of its nuclear and other arsenals under UN supervision. However, arms sales continue, including both high-technology systems and relatively simple equipment. The sale of the South African G5 howitzer to the Gulf States demonstrates that the region remains an attractive market for Third World suppliers of less technologically advanced weapons. In addition, there have been efforts to improve indigenous production capabilities, particularly in Israel, in Iraq before the Gulf War, in Egypt, Syria and Iran. Defence expenditures remain high: for example, amounting to £3 billion in Israel, 12 per cent of Gross Domestic Product. Weapons purchases are increasing: "Syria is estimated to be spending more than £1 billion on buying about 600 T72 tanks from Russia and Czechoslovakia, artillery from Bulgaria, and surface-to-surface SCUD missiles from North Korea. Iran is steadily rebuilding its military, which was seriously damaged in the war with Iraq, by spending more than £1 billion a year on buying Russian aircraft and tanks and it is still holding 115 Iraqi aircraft from the Gulf War ... Saudi Arabia is attempting to purchase 72 new F15s, in addition to the £15–20 billion Tornado deal it has already concluded with Britain. Egypt has bought 555 American-made Abrahams M1-A1 tanks, which it is assembling itself, as well as buying F16 fighters assembled in Turkey."[19] The persistence of Arab-Israeli rivalries, Arab-Arab frictions, and anticipated Arab-Iranian-Turkish competition in former Soviet Central Asia, are key issues which require resolution as any part of any effective regional arms control regime. Their intractability vividly demonstrates the difficulties with this approach.

Some have proposed drawing on the experience derived from the European 'Helsinki process' to engineer a lowering of tension and eventual resolution of conflicts. Steps proposed include: promoting information exchange on forces and readiness levels, notification of manoeuvres, limits on naval manoeuvres, use of UN-controlled demilitarised zones on disputed borders, and the creation of a permanent commission of all Middle Eastern states to investigate violations of the peace. However, many question the appropriateness of the model, noting that the Helsinki process itself brought real benefits only *after* a genuine climate of confidence and co-operation had developed with the fall of Communist regimes in Eastern Europe. An alternative proposal involves the creation of a Mediterranean regime, including Israel and Syria, to examine functional issues of mutual interest, for example the management of water supplies, migration, and environmental issues. Again, it is doubtful whether such a process could be sufficiently robust to bring about genuine reconciliation and eventual peace.

The opportunities offered by supply-side approaches seem similarly meagre; the UN Arms Transfer Register, possible creation of a UN arms control agency, a strengthening and formalising through a treaty of the Missile Technology Control Regime, the introduction of a classification system for 'offensive' and 'defensive' weapons systems, and tighter export controls on particular classes of weapons, have all been suggested. Each proposal has been criticised, and indeed rejected by some, as being inadequate for the task in hand. However, this is to under-estimate their value

---

[19] Richard Beeston, "Middle East Flocks to Arms Bazaar", *The Times,* 12 May 1992.

and to evade a central premise of arms control: that small incremental steps should be used to build confidence, reduce friction, and to moderate, if not reduce, dependence on military power to assure security. The admitted difficulty of the problem is not an excuse for inaction.

It is important to note the recent decision of the five UN Security Council members, coincidentally the major arms supplying countries in the world, to co-operate in restricting arms sales to the Middle East. While little concrete has been achieved as yet, and China appears unlikely to give full collaboration, some self-restraint by the G5 may be in prospect. Success for this initiative would represent a major advance.

The Impact of Arms Control Agreements

Recent arms control successes, including the negotiation of START and US-Russian bilateral agreements on nuclear and chemical weapons, are a direct result of the ending of Cold War confrontation. Progress at the multilateral level has also been encouraging: a Chemical Weapons Convention will probably be signed in 1992; the 1975 Biological Weapons Convention was strengthened further by the 1991 Review Conference; progress is being made to ensure the extension of the Nuclear Non-Proliferation Treaty in 1995. This generally positive picture has been reinforced by the successful negotiation of the Conventional Forces in Europe Treaty (CFE), the growing number of countries signing up to the Missile Technology Control Regime (MTCR), and by successful efforts to maintain the relevance of the Co-ordinating Committee for Multilateral Export Control Regime (COCOM). However, this generally positive picture masks considerable problems, particularly with the agreements relating to conventional weapons: CFE, MTCR and COCOM.

While CFE remains a considerable achievement, the break-up of the Soviet Union means that many of the new states in the East have as yet failed to ratify the Treaty. Many argue that without ratification, the basis for NATO country reductions in military forces is severely undermined, and that failure to ratify in the East should prompt rethinking in the West. Others note that economic problems and current trends in military planning in the East point towards substantial reductions of former Soviet Union and WTO forces, whether the Treaty is ratified or not. However, all Western observers agree on the importance of the Treaty to promote political stability through the implementation of agreed verification procedures and information exchange. There is little doubt that widespread non-adherence to the Treaty would undermine severely the progress made in building up confidence between old adversaries. It is for this reason that the CSCE meetings in July 1992 were concerned with ensuring that the Treaty is verified. This said, the lack of qualitative controls in the Treaty is a major drawback requiring further consideration.

The MTCR has been successful in slowing proliferation and the indigenous development of 'Third World' ballistic missile systems. Several key and potential suppliers have recently been persuaded to accept MTCR restrictions, including for example Israel, Argentina, Brazil and China, although it remains to be seen whether these commitments will be carried out in practice. However, it is unlikely that the Regime will *prevent* proliferation in the long term. For example, while existing Russian policy is cautious about missile sales, ending the supply of SCUD missiles to Afghanistan in January 1992, such sales may yet be resumed given the country's economic problems. Yet, for the moment, sales remain restricted and the MTCR demonstrates that supply-side restraint is possible when sales of particular systems are deemed to respresent a *direct* threat to the security of the producing states.

The continued relevance and efficacy of the COCOM arrangement has also been questioned following the break-up of the Warsaw Pact. Many observers are pressing for an increase in the transfer of advanced technology to the new democacies in the East, rather than its restriction. "These changing perceptions led to substantial changes agreed at the high level COCOM Consultative Group Meeting in Paris on 24 May 1992. The international list of 116 categories was cut by roughly 65 per cent and restructured into a new 'core list' of nine categories which stress advanced electronics, materials, computers and propulsion technology. Czechoslovakia, Hungary and Poland received further dispensations ..."[20] Some continue to have reservations, arguing that COCOM must continue because: a) Russia does not need advanced technology in the early stages of economic reconstruction and defence conversion, b) Russia remains dominated by former Communist officials who may yet return to power and misuse the technology acquired, c) the restrictions help to prevent transfer of advanced technology to potential proliferators via the former Eastern Bloc. It seems unlikely that COCOM will be reoriented to control exports to the Third World.[21]

Given these modest arms control successes, what approach should be taken in the future? Clearly the achievements of the past must be consolidated, for example through ratification of existing treaties and strengthening their provisions where possible. In an increasingly multipolar world and with multiple sources of arms supply, themselves less restrained by the influence of the former Cold War super-powers, effective arms control arrangements and/or treaties will need to be more multilateral. Three possibilities currently being explored are: expansion of the UN Register of Conventional Arms Transfers, the development of regional collective security arrangements similar to CSCE/CFE; and establishing a 'Conventional Weapons Prevention Treaty' (CPT) similar to the NPT and/or the anticipated Chemical Weapons Convention.

> The problems with these approaches are clear. An expanded UN Register could indeed introduce greater openness and make it easier to monitor excessive arms build-ups in particular countries, but the next vital step still has to be taken of establishing the role the UN is to play when such build-ups are monitored and the suppliers of the arms identified. It is unclear how far and under what circumstances the international community is prepared to act, including the possible use of military force, to deter or curtail

---

[20] "Responses to Weapons Proliferation", in *Strategic Survey 1991–92*, The International Institute for Strategic Studies, p. 203.
[21] For arguments in support of this view see *ibid.*

such activity. The Iraqi example may yet prove to be a 'one-off action'.

The use of the 'CSCE-CFE' model outside Europe depends on agreed political solutions to an area's conflicts: it is no accident that CFE success was based on an already existing East-West rapprochement.

The negotiation of a CPT is certainly a long-term prospect, and the eventual introduction of such a regime will almost certainly require concerted action by the current UN Security Council permanent members. This seems a dim prospect given both Western and Eastern propensity to export conventional arms and recent decisions in Russia to pursue actively such a policy: "officials in Russia, Ukraine, Belarus and other former Soviet republics make so secret of the desire to develop China as a lucrative market for their excess advanced weapons. Mikhail Maley, a senior adviser to Mr Yeltsin, bluntly told the *Rossiiskaya Gazeta* in Moscow a few months ago that the attempt to convert Russia's arms plants into consumer goods factories had failed. 'Conversion should be a transformation of the military industrial complex into an export industry,' he said. In March, Pyotr Aven, Russia's Minister of Foreign Economic Relations, visited Beijing and proclaimed on returning home that he had signed arms contracts with the Chinese. On May 19, Mr Yeltsin told defence plant managers that Russia would try to market $5 billion-worth of arms yearly."[22] Such views are echoed by Western companies, who are supported by their respective governments as they compete in other potentially lucrative markets.

In spite of these sales, which will involve proliferation of conventional weapons of increasingly high quality and capability, some argue that "there is ground for cautious optimism. In most

---

[22] Jim Hoagland, "Russian Arms to China: Japan Steps In", *International Herald Tribune,* 14 July 1992.

cases control regimes already exist and can be made better, and solutions exist even to some of the most difficult proliferation dangers", but they note "the real solution to proliferation control, however, involves regional conflict resolution, crisis prevention, confidence-building and arms control. When regional actors resolve the disputes that motivate their most destabilising weapons projects they accomplish more than the most elaborate non-proliferation systems."[23] If it is true that proliferation can only be stopped by containing demand, efforts to influence supplier behaviour must be geared to providing the breathing space required for the negotiation of necessary political solutions. *If* Western governments can restrain their own companies, will they be able to persuade the FSU and former WTO states to do the same to meet a theoretical joint interest in reducing proliferation? Persuasion alone appears unlikely to succeed unless backed by the 'threat' of aid conditionality. But even this threat may be ineffective. Western aid has to be sufficient to make a difference to development in the first place before its threatened withdrawal can influence policy-makers; because aid on such a scale appears to be unlikely for other reasons, conditionality will be ineffective.

Aid Conditionality Revisited

Japanese concern neatly demonstrates the problem. It has been reported that: "the Japanese Government has launched a secret diplomatic initiative to limit Moscow's arms sales to Beijing's Communist Government. Japan is quietly warning Russia that upsetting the military balance in Asia by strengthening China with high-tech conventional weaponry will damage Moscow's chances for massive economic aid from Japan and the West for reconstruction, despite the encouraging noises made at the Group of Seven Summit in Munich. ..."[24] Sales of modern Russian aircraft, and rumours of Chinese interest in buying an aircraft carrier being constructed in the Ukraine, are particularly disturbing for the Japanese. Yet, Japanese linkage of aid to arms sales

---

[23] *Strategic Survey, 1991–92*, p. 211.
[24] Jim Hoagland, "Russian Arms to China: Japan Steps In", *International Herald Tribune*, 14 July 1992.

seems unlikely to be persuasive given their repeated statements that such aid will not be forthcoming in any case until the dispute over the Kurile Islands is settled. Similarly, US and Western exhortations for Russian arms sales restraint are likely to be unsuccessful unless the many widely publicised reservations about granting such aid are overcome. This is not to argue that massive aid should be offered to ensure that conditionality works. It does demonstrate, however, that for the West to have influence, aid and technological assistance must be given. A combination of severe East European economic problems and grudging Western financial assistance represents a recipe for increased 'Eastern' arms sales, which Western governments will be poorly placed to influence.

5 Conclusions

Declining domestic markets for conventional arms in the 'developed' world have forced the defence industries in both East and West to adjust. In the West this is proving to be an uncomfortable but manageable problem, while the economic woes of the East are such that successful restructuring will be exceedingly difficult. The immediate aftermath of the end of the Cold War has seen continued efforts to export large quantities of conventional weapons. While Western and Eastern governments have collaborated extensively to prevent exports of weapons of mass destruction and related technologies, the competition to export conventional weapons has not been similarly restricted.

The economic imperatives driving Western companies and Eastern military industries alike mean that these suppliers will be ready to meet the demands of states wishing to purchase advanced weaponry; the lesson that unilateral restraint merely offers opportunities to competitors remains engrained. Competition will be made all the fiercer by reductions in the size of the global market.

The difficulties of 'conversion' to civilian uses are considerable and efforts in this direction will bring positive results only in the medium to long-term. Thus, arms sales seem certain to continue in the meantime, being constrained mainly by the procurers' ability to pay and the level and number of regional conflicts and antagonisms fuelling local arms races. It is the reductions in conflicts and thus in demand which will force industries, whether Eastern or Western, to restructure their activities and concentrate on 'civilian' production. In an increasingly unstable world the prospects are indeed gloomy.

While FSU and former WTO countries will continue to export arms, the reduction of their domestic markets will be crippling to defence industries and large scale closures and redundancies seem assured, given the difficulties of conversion and indeed the *inability* of many to restructure. This will generate instability in the East. Even if 'demand reduction' efforts fail 'Third World' markets will not be large enough to provide work for redundant FSU defence facilities.

The prospect of continued instability in the former Eastern Bloc and in the Third World prompts the question: what should the 'West' do? Can it stand aside or must it intervene actively: whether through economic aid and assistance, developing both supply-side and demand-side arms control regimes, or with armed force when feasible and appropriate? These are not new questions but standing aside is clearly not an option. Aid may seem wasteful, arms control painfully slow, and military involvement unpalatable in the extreme, but the last is infinitely worse than the alternatives. Western aid and involvement is essential; sufficient and adequately funded efforts are required to 'buy' genuine security; the alternatives are too bleak to accept.

List of Participants

AMMON, Peter: Ministry of Foreign Affairs, Bonn
ANTHONY, Ian: SIPRI, Stockholm
ARKWRIGHT, Paul: Foreign and Commonwealth Office, London
BAND, Stephen: Standard and Sheffield Investment Corporation, Washington D.C.

BEACH, General Sir Hugh: Council for Arms Control, London
BISCHAK, Gregory: National Commission for Economic Conversion and Disarmament, Washington D.C.
BLUTH, Christoph: University of Essex, Colchester
CORNISH, Paul: Foreign and Commonwealth Office, London
DAHINDEN, Martin: Federal Department of Foreign Affairs, Bern
DENTON, Geoffrey: Wilton Park
DONNELLY, Brian: Foreign and Commonwealth Office, London
EHTESHAMI, Anoushiravan: University of Essex
GOLDEN, James: US Military Academy, West Point
HOENKAMP, Coen: Ministry of Defence, The Hague
HOLMBOE, Rolf: Ministry of Foreign Affairs, Copenhagen
KENNAWAY, Alexander: Imperial College, London
KIRK, Matthew: Foreign and Commonwealth Office, London
LATTER, Richard: Wilton Park
MATSUI, Yasuo: Japanese Delegation to the OECD, Paris
von MORR, Hubertus: Federal Chancellory, Bonn
MÜLLER, Dieter: Berlin-Brandenberg Institute of Foreign Affairs, Potsdam
NATHAN, Robert: Nathan Associates Inc, Arlington
NEWTON, Verne: Franklin D Roosevelt Library, New York
PELLERIN, Alain: NATO Defence College, Rome
RENNER, Michael: The World Watch Institute, Washington D.C.
STSEPINSKY, Youri: Russian Institute for Strategic Studies, Moscow
TARRY, Nicholas: BBC Monitoring, Caversham
WALINSKY, Adam: Advisor to US Congress on the Personnel Dimension of Defence Conversion, Washington D.C.
YOUNGER, Alex: Foreign and Commonwealth Office, London

Printed in the United Kingdom for HMSO
Dd294513 9/92 C6 G3397 10170